BLISS

(Félicité)

Plays by Caryl Churchill published by TCG

Blue Heart

Cloud 9

A Dream Play
(adapted from August Strindberg)

Drunk Enough to Say I Love You?

Light Shining in Buckinghamshire

Mad Forest

A Number

The Skriker

This is a Chair

BLISS

(Félicité)

Olivier Choinière

Translated by Caryl Churchill

THEATRE COMMUNICATIONS GROUP NEW YORK 2009

The original French-language production of *Félicité* was first presented at Théâtre La Liscorne, Montreal, Canada, on 16 October 2007, with the following cast:

COSMETIC SALESPERSON   Muriel Dutil
DISPLAY ASSISTANT   Maxime Denommée
MANAGER   Roger La Rue
ORACLE   Isabelle Roy

Director   Sylvain Bélanger
Set Designer   Pierre-Étienne Locas
Costume Designer   Sarah Balleux
Lighting Designer   Martin Labrecque
Composer   Larsen Lupin

It was a Théâtre de la Manufacture production, under the artistic direction of Jean-Denis Leduc

This translation of *Bliss* was first performed at the Royal Court Theatre Upstairs, London, on 28 March 2008, with the following cast:

ORACLE	Hayley Carmichael
COSMETIC SALESPERSON	Brid Brennan
DISPLAY ASSISTANT	Justin Salinger
MANAGER	Neil Dudgeon

Director	Joe Hill-Gibbins
Designer	Jeremy Herbert
Lighting Designer	Nigel Edwards
Sound Designer	Christopher Shutt

BLISS

(Félicité)

BLISS / *perfect joy or happiness; the state of being in heaven*

The alienation of the spectator which reinforces the contemplated objects (a result of his own unconscious activity) works like this: the more he contemplates, the less he lives; the more he identifies with the dominant images of need, the less he understands his own life and his own desires. The spectacle's estrangement from the acting subject appears in the fact that the individual's gestures are no longer his own; they are the gestures of someone else who represents them to him. The spectator does not feel at home anywhere, because the spectacle is everywhere.

Guy Debord, *The Society of Spectacle*

4

Characters

COSMETICS SALESPERSON, *1. Acts under another's direction. 2. Applies make-up, disguises, smoothes things over. 3. Woman late forties.*

MANAGER, *1. Runs things on behalf of someone else. 2. Organises, forbids, confronts. 3. Man early fifties.*

DISPLAY ASSISTANT, *1. Designs and arranges the displays, shows off the merchandise. 2. Records, places, situates. 3. Man late twenties.*

ORACLE, *1. Expresses herself with authority, is highly trusted. 2. Announces, decides, settles. 3. Woman early thirties.*

Place

The stage, that is *from the other side of the mirror*.

Punctuation

A slash (/) indicates the start of the next speech.

The dash (–) indicates a gesture expressing a thought, an ellipse, hesitation or censorship.

A sentence without a full stop (.) indicates that the next speech follows without a pause.

Note

Capital letters indicate a louder voice or a quote from a newspaper.

MANAGER, COSMETICS SALESPERSON, DISPLAY ASSISTANT *enter and face the audience. They're wearing blue overalls, except for the* MANAGER. *They're all wearing nametags with letters and numbers backwards so you can't read them. They're smiling.* ORACLE *enters and faces the audience. She's not smiling. She's wearing the same blue overalls. On her nametag you can read:* ORACLE 31

ORACLE   Begin.

COSMETICS   Everyone – breathless

DISPLAY   Your legs –

MANAGER   No one dared breathe

COSMETICS   The silence – at the end of the note, I mean when the last note had died away

MANAGER   Vast

DISPLAY   Then everyone looked up at the same time

MANAGER   The balloons were beginning to fall

COSMETICS   RAINING balloons

MANAGER   But she stayed where she was, microphone in her hand, mouth open – eyes scrunched up

COSMETICS   And it's as if – she was still singing

DISPLAY   That's right: as if the roar of the crowd was coming out of her mouth

MANAGER   Thousands of spectators – in her mouth

COSMETICS   People were yelling, balloons still raining
              down on them – on her, standing there

MANAGER   Mouth open – eyes scrunched up

DISPLAY   And then flash – all at once, from all over

MANAGER   Wonderful

DISPLAY   As if everyone wanted to keep the same
               memory.

COSMETICS   After that, she lowered her arms, she
              opened her eyes, she smiled – yes, she
              smiled and she said: 'Thank you'

ORACLE   No – before

COSMETICS   Before what?

ORACLE   Before she said it

MANAGER   You're right – before that, she put her
               hand on her heart and said: 'Thank you,'
               but / without saying thank you

DISPLAY   WITHOUT saying thank you

MANAGER   Just mouthing the words 'Thank you'

DISPLAY   Yes, because people –

COSMETICS   But she did end up saying 'Thank you,' I
              mean really

DISPLAY   But it took – That's why she said: 'Stop.
               It's too much.'

COSMETICS   YES, then after that: 'I love you lots!' –
              with her arm

DISPLAY	Then: 'I love you too,' because everyone was shouting: 'I LOVE YOU'
MANAGER	'WE LOVE YOU, CÉLINE!'
COSMETICS	Then Céline crying
DISPLAY	On the big screen: close-up of Céline's face
MANAGER	One tear – with her finger. Fantastic – wonderful
DISPLAY	But everyone kept on: 'CÉLINE! CÉLINE!'
COSMETICS	That's when Céline said: 'Thank you from the bottom of my heart,' bending her head, then softly, the first notes of – obviously! For an encore Céline sang 'The Power of Love', still crying
MANAGER	Her cheeks – soaking wet
COSMETICS	And everyone was crying. After the encore: 'DON'T GO, / CÉLINE!'
DISPLAY	CÉLINE on television – in every house
COSMETICS	In the living room: everyone crying
DISPLAY	Next day – newspapers, magazines: 'GOODBYE, CÉLINE', in big letters
ORACLE	Not 'GOODBYE', 'SEE YOU LATER'
MANAGER	'SEE YOU LATER' – yes, that's right – Céline just wanted a break.
COSMETICS	When Céline appeared at the press conference in jeans and a sweater – a

baggy sweater, really – simple. The journalists were on their knees

DISPLAY   The Photographer wanted to take a photo but he was crying too much

COSMETICS   Céline and René sat down. Céline smiled – simple. And the press officer had a word with the Journalist and the Journalist asked if – no – earlier, the Journalist said: 'Hello, Céline,' and Céline said: 'Hello, lovely. How's your throat?' Céline knew the Journalist had been ill, she'd been briefed – no – she / just knew

MANAGER   And what did the Journalist ask?

COSMETICS   The Journalist asked: 'How long's the break for, Céline?' And René replied

MANAGER   It's not René who replied, it's Céline – she replied: 'I don't know yet' and after that René said: 'Maybe two – three years'

DISPLAY   That's right: 'Maybe five, maybe seven'

COSMETICS   'Or maybe not, maybe just a month, who knows,' but 'If Céline took a break for a month it would feel like ten years, if she came back after ten years it would be as if she'd never left,' thought the Journalist

MANAGER   Céline said: 'I want to take some time for myself, with my family,' then gazing upward: 'One thing I do know, I'll always be with you'

COSMETICS   And the Journalist felt she was speaking

to her – for her – that it was just to her she was saying that

DISPLAY When Céline got up from the press table, the Photographer felt she turned towards him, it was for him she was turning her head, stroking her belly

COSMETICS Céline was pregnant

ORACLE Céline didn't say she was pregnant

MANAGER No, not at the press conference, it was a fucking journalist who

COSMETICS The Journalist didn't say anything, I mean she just THOUGHT Céline was pregnant – maybe, even if deep down she knew

MANAGER Someone talked, someone took a photo, a photo of her lying in bed

DISPLAY It wasn't one of the Photographer's photos

MANAGER René made them withdraw the magazine with the photo – all the magazines, from all the newsagents and all the shops. Céline wanted it to be INTIMATE.

DISPLAY It was in the plane – René's private jet 'the Céline', that the Photographer – knew. It was unbelievable! The Photographer had always dreamt of flying in 'the Céline', and it was there, up in the sky, Céline asked him: 'How'd you like to be my motherhood photographer?' and the Photographer cried

MANAGER   She wanted to take the time to experience it together, peacefully

COSMETICS The Journalist had obtained an exclusive interview with Céline in 'the Céline', and when they landed Céline said: 'Why don't you come and spend some time at the house?' She didn't need to say any more

MANAGER   She wanted it to be at home, just the family

COSMETICS So when Céline took the Journalist's hand and looked at her with – her eyes, she knew what Céline was going to tell her and the Journalist cried

MANAGER   And when the Californian Doctor said: 'Céline, you'll have to remain in bed,' Céline didn't feel like a prisoner, quite the opposite, she said to herself: 'I'm going to stay in bed and I'm going to read, read all the fan letters I haven't had time to read' and all day long she lay there in the bedroom, a wonderful bedroom

DISPLAY   The light was – extraordinary

MANAGER   Even bigger than the bedroom when she was married, the second time

COSMETICS Maybe not bigger

MANAGER   She wanted it just as big

DISPLAY   It wasn't bigger but it seemed bigger – because of the desert

COSMETICS   The desert?

DISPLAY   The bedroom was at the back of the house – looked out onto the desert. The view – unbelievable

COSMETICS   And the garden – the / Babylonian garden

DISPLAY   Babylonian

MANAGER   The Las Vegas house: a real castle

DISPLAY   The Photographer took photos

COSMETICS   That bedroom – maybe not quite as big as the second marriage bedroom – was where she invited the Journalist

MANAGER   No journalist has been in Céline's bedroom. Céline said to René: 'I don't want anyone – except my friends and family.' Journalists just saw PHOTOS / of the bedroom

COSMETICS   Not all the journalists, THE Journalist

ORACLE   The Biographer

MANAGER   OK, the Biographer, because journalists, journalists in general, they come to press conferences or they can fuck off

COSMETICS   The Biographer

MANAGER   Even when they come to press conferences – you've got to watch out who you ask to press conferences. You remember the French journalist / who

COSMETICS   You don't ask just anyone

MANAGER   Exactly – the French journalist who said to René: 'Céline? You mean Louis-Fernand Céline?'

COSMETICS   'Ferdinand' – oh god, yes

MANAGER   'Louis-Ferdinand Céline?'

DISPLAY   Who is Louis-Ferdinand Céline?

COSMETICS   An actor

MANAGER   And René said: 'No, not Louis-Ferdinand, but Céline, THE CÉLINE, the one and ONLY,' then everyone laughed and the stupid fucking French journalist shut his fucking stupid French gob.

COSMETICS   I say 'journalist' because at first she couldn't believe she'd been made THE official Biographer, I mean that Céline had given her a gift like that. When she said: 'I want people to know the truth,' she was so beautiful – radiant. The Biographer replied: 'Céline, spiteful people are unhappy people.'

DISPLAY   She was so beautiful – radiant, lying in that vast bed, her hair spread out on the pillows – a mountain of pillows and her on top

MANAGER   Wonderful

DISPLAY   And the Photographer asked René to lie down beside her, in his golden pyjamas

MANAGER   It wasn't pyjamas. It was traditional / dress

DISPLAY   Traditional dress, but I said pyjamas
              because it was so – simple, so lovely to
              see them, to suddenly see the man and
              the woman, like any other couple waking
              up, 'CÉLINE AND RENÉ HAVE A
              LIE-IN', said the caption. Parents-to-be
              who love each other and are looking
              forward to their baby

COSMETICS   Céline said: 'I want my child to know
              how much he was loved and wanted and
              looked forward to, how much his father
              loved his mother and his mother loved
              his father, how much the whole family
              loved each other and were looking
              forward to his arrival.' And the
              Biographer cried

DISPLAY   The Photographer saw before him the
              teenager who sang for the Pope, he saw
              before him THE VOICE OF GOD, the
              most beautiful voice in the world, the
              Photographer had in his viewfinder
              success and international triumph, but
              when success and international triumph
              said to him: 'How do you want me?' as if
              she'd never done it before, almost
              blushing as if it was the first time, then
              the Photographer saw before him THE
              LITTLE GIRL FROM
              CHARLEMAGNE, the childhood friend
              he'd been at school with, and the
              Photographer cried.

MANAGER   René came in one morning with some
              magazines from Quebec. Céline adored

	reading magazines from Quebec. When René came into the bedroom, Céline said: 'Darling, come and kiss me.'
ORACLE	No – she says: 'Thanks for the flowers. They smell good.'
COSMETICS	What flowers?
ORACLE	The flowers René sent
MANAGER	/ René never
ORACLE	BECAUSE he went out early to play golf AND he wasn't going to be there when Céline woke up. The Chambermaid puts them in a vase
DISPLAY	What Chambermaid?
ORACLE	The black Chambermaid
MANAGER	René didn't hire a black chambermaid
ORACLE	ONE of the chambermaids out of a whole lot of chambermaids, René can't be expected to know all the chambermaids. The black Chambermaid puts the flowers on the chest of drawers, next to the mirror, with a card signed: 'With Love, René', and goes to give Céline a letter
COSMETICS	What letter?
ORACLE	A fan letter
COSMETICS	But it's usually the secretary who gets / the letters
ORACLE	Too late. Céline says: 'Give it to me.'

COSMETICS   What does the letter say?

ORACLE   The letter says: 'Dear Céline, I think
            about you a lot. Like you, I'm always in
            bed. My illness stops me getting up. My
            family look after me. When I'm sad they
            play me your music. I like the song 'I See
            You Everywhere' very much. It's like me
            talking but you singing. I hope I'll get
            better one day so I can see one of your
            concerts live. Love you lots, Isabelle.'
            Before leaving, the Chambermaid asks
            Céline for her autograph.

MANAGER   'There's two kinds of employee,' thinks
            René

ORACLE   Céline signs an autograph for her – in
            French

MANAGER   'There's the ones that ask for autographs
            and the ones that don't – simple as that'

ORACLE   The black Chambermaid goes out of
            the room backwards – big smile –
            disappears.

DISPLAY   Then the Bodyguard doesn't see anyone
            leave?

ORACLE   The Bodyguard's in the staff kitchen –
            having lunch.

DISPLAY   He might hear – I don't know – the door
            opening or shutting

ORACLE   If the Bodyguard heard the door he'd
            think it was the Biographer who'd just
            gone in

COSMETICS Isn't the Biographer in the bedroom
           ALREADY?

ORACLE   NO – the Biographer hasn't arrived yet.
           Céline's all alone – crying.

MANAGER   René comes into the bedroom with some
           magazines from Quebec – where you can
           see the photos of Céline and René in the
           bedroom and read the articles about
           Céline's pregnancy, but when René sees
           Céline crying, René thinks: 'Bad news.'

COSMETICS Céline's crying about the letter, I mean
           she found it so beautiful – touching

MANAGER   It's when Céline says: 'Thanks for the
           flowers. They smell good,' when he sees
           the flowers, that's when he thinks: 'Bad
           news.' He's really scared, because René
           never sent Céline any flowers. He goes to
           look at the flowers by the mirror. An
           enormous bunch because of the reflection.
           He picks up the card 'With love, René.'
           His accountant has already told him his
           signature's easy to imitate. He doesn't say
           anything about it to Céline, he goes out of
           the bedroom with the card – goes to see
           Céline's personal Bodyguard

DISPLAY   The Bodyguard doesn't understand, he
           didn't see anyone

MANAGER   René says: 'Go check the flowers.'

DISPLAY   The Bodyguard comes into the room and
           goes to look at the flowers, even though
           it's not his job – bends over them. Céline

says: 'They smell good,' but the flowers hardly smell at all and anyway they're a long way from the bed. The Bodyguard says to himself: 'How could she smell the flowers from way over there?'

MANAGER   The Californian Doctor has forbidden Céline to get out of bed. 'It's dangerous. Céline could lose her baby.' René gets out his mobile to call the florist and find out who they sold the flowers to, but there's no number on the card because it's not a florist's card, it's a label from Wal-Mart

COSMETICS   When the Biographer comes into the bedroom, Céline says: 'I've had such a beautiful letter – really touching, I'd like to reply, I really want to write to her.' There's no return address on the envelope, there's nothing at all on the envelope because there isn't an envelope, there's just the letter. Céline says to the Biographer: 'I want to know all about Isabelle,' smiling through her tears

ORACLE   No – crying

COSMETICS   Crying?

ORACLE   Howling – with pain

MANAGER   René runs into the bedroom

ORACLE   René's nowhere near the bedroom, he's outside – the other end of the garden

MANAGER   René's calling the DOCTOR

ORACLE   The Doctor's already in the bedroom –
            with the Biographer and the Bodyguard.
            Céline's howling

DISPLAY   The Bodyguard goes nearer

MANAGER   The Doctor's running to the bed

ORACLE   Céline's covers are stained with blood –
            between her thighs

MANAGER   They lift up the covers

COSMETICS   The Biographer closes her eyes – takes
            Céline's hand – René plunges his head /
            between her thighs

MANAGER   The DOCTOR

COSMETICS   I mean the DOCTOR – the
            CALIFORNIAN Doctor plunges his
            head between Céline's thighs

DISPLAY   Céline's cries are like a song. You'd think
            she was singing. The Bodyguard backs
            away

MANAGER   The Doctor shouts: 'SHE'S LOSING
            HER BABY.'

COSMETICS   The Biographer picks up the phone – to
            call an ambulance

MANAGER   The Doctor hangs up the phone. He
            snarls: 'Imbecile! She can't move.'

DISPLAY   The Bodyguard bumps into the chest of
            drawers and things fall off the top: CDs,
            a camera

COSMETICS   The Biographer doesn't know what to

do, she starts wiping the blood – on the phone

MANAGER   'CALL RENÉ!'

DISPLAY   The Bodyguard sees in the Doctor's blood red hands, Céline's blood red baby

COSMETICS   It's not even a baby, it's hardly a baby, it's – the Biographer can't look, the Biographer goes out, the Nurse comes in – it's a big red prawn. Céline's personal Nurse takes the big red prawn out of the Doctor's hands

DISPLAY   The Bodyguard can't look

COSMETICS   The Nurse doesn't know what to do with it

ORACLE   The flash goes off

COSMETICS   What flash?

ORACLE   The flash from the camera.

MANAGER   Who's taking PHOTOS?

DISPLAY   NO ONE!

COSMETICS   The Nurse throws the big prawn down the toilet – flush! – gets a towel, wets it, wrings it – washes Céline, changes Céline

DISPLAY   The Bodyguard puts back the camera, the CDs – he's shaking

MANAGER   The Californian Doctor calls René – he says: 'René, I'm so sorry. The baby's dead.' René's shaking – his legs won't hold him any more, he's come all the way across the garden. He runs into the

house, holding himself up on the walls,
makes it to the bedroom, his eyes –
burning with tears. René wants to tear
his heart out, Céline keeps saying:
'DOCTOR, WHERE'S MY BABY? MY
BABY?'

COSMETICS Finally Céline goes to sleep. The Nurse
stays with her – the rest of the day – all
night. Next morning, Céline wakes up
with a big smile, then she says to the
Nurse: 'Mum, I'm so glad you came to
see me.' Céline's sick, she's / not well

MANAGER She just needs to see her family, to have
them around her. René calls Céline's
Mother and her brothers and sisters –
her Father. He tells them to come. He
doesn't say why, he just tells them to
come, and when the family get to Vegas
next day, René takes Céline's Mother in
his arms and cries

COSMETICS René doesn't have to say anything,
Céline's Mother knows

MANAGER René cries on her shoulder. Behind
Céline's Mother is Céline's Father. René
looks at Céline's Father, smiling, shy,
awkward, overcome by René, Vegas, by
the marble, the soft tops, the sunshine,
the garden, the desert, the palm trees.
How can the Father smile? His
daughter's lost her baby – their baby, and
René closes his eyes, hugs Céline's
Mother tight as if to stop himself from

COSMETICS   Céline's Mother says to René: 'I know what it's like, I lost my first one.' The Mother goes into the house, goes straight to the Nurse to find out how Céline is. The Nurse says: 'Take care of her.' Céline's Mother doesn't need anyone telling her that. She knows perfectly well how to look after her daughter.

DISPLAY   The Bodyguard squeezes up to let Céline's Brother come in. Céline's Brother is surprised that the Bodyguard is as – small as him. The Brother sits on the bed and hugs his sister, Céline, who he hasn't seen for ages, except on stage or in photos, and she looks younger than in her photos – or thinner, he can't tell which. He doesn't know what to say. He just feels awkward, awkward at being alone with her, and she's smiling – the others still haven't come – the rest of the family. She strokes his arm, she says: 'I think about the sick children and I don't feel so bad,' but he can't look at her any more – he looks away, has a look round. Unbelievable. He'd imagined a much bigger bedroom – that's it: the room looked bigger in the pictures. If he'd brought some magazines from Quebec he could have compared. He stares at the flowers, the flowers by the mirror. He gets up – the bunch looks twice as big because of the mirror. He bends over the flowers. The flowers don't smell. They're plastic.

COSMETICS   When Céline's Mother goes into the kitchen, the famous kitchen in the Vegas house, the kitchen she's only seen in pictures – in the magazines, she sees dirty dishes spilling all over the worktop. Céline's Mother's annoyed to see dirty dishes on the worktop, I mean that no one had thought of putting them in the dishwasher. Céline's Mother picks up a dirty plate to put it in the dishwasher but she can't find a dishwasher. Where is the dishwasher? Where are the staff, the maid, the cook? She calls René, she's going out of the kitchen calling René, she starts wandering down the corridors calling René, she starts thinking: 'The man I gave my daughter to,' she's thinking about her daughter, she thinks: 'I haven't been to see my daughter yet'

MANAGER   Céline says to her Father: 'Don't cry, Pops. It could have been worse.' Céline's Father doesn't understand what she means. What could have been worse? 'There are people with nothing, nothing at all' – she repeats: 'Nothing at all,' and Céline's Father understands less than ever. His son's at the other end of the bedroom. He doesn't say anything, he stays there without moving. You'd think he was hiding something behind his back. Where are the others? His brothers and sisters? And then Céline's Father sees what the Brother was hiding behind his back, he puts it up to his face: a camera – he's going to take a photo, it's really not a good moment. Céline's Father says to Céline's Brother: 'Put on a record,' and the Brother backs off

DISPLAY   The Brother puts the camera down – a throwaway camera he bought at a tax-free shop. He puts it on the chest of drawers, he's glad to get rid of it, he feels silly for having bought it. He wipes his hands on his thighs and picks up a CD, the first one he finds, one of Céline's early singles. He picks up another one, a Céline double album, because there's only Céline CDs in Céline's bedroom.

ORACLE   She says: 'Put some Céline on for me.'

MANAGER   The song begins and Céline cuddles up against her Father. Céline's Father daren't take his daughter in his arms. She puts her head on his knees. She says: 'Stroke my hair like when I was sick.'

COSMETICS   Céline's Mother hears the music, a song she knows – which her daughter sings – used to sing, she walks towards the music

MANAGER   Céline's sucking her thumb and humming like when she was little, which used to make her Father say: 'One day she'll be a singer'

ORACLE   'One day she'll suck cocks.'

COSMETICS   Cé – Céline's Mother stops at the door

MANAGER   Her Father daren't move, his arms by his sides

COSMETICS   The Mother listens to Céline singing, hears the music – her husband, her son

MANAGER   Céline's hugging him tight now – presses against him as if she'd like to go back inside him, give him the strength to hug her

DISPLAY   Céline's Brother's looking at the photos, the newspaper cuttings, the posters of Céline on Céline's bedroom wall, her Brother wants to sink through the floor

COSMETICS   Céline's mother puts her hand on the doorknob

MANAGER   Someone could, someone's going to, someone wants to, Céline's Father wants to sink through the floor

ORACLE   Doorbell.

COSMETICS   Céline's Mother freezes, turns round, walks down the corridor, goes towards the front door – stops. She's waiting for someone to open it – someone who lives there – staff. Céline's Mother calls out: 'IS SOMEONE GOING TO OPEN THE DOOR?'

ORACLE   Doorbell.

COSMETICS   'NOBODY'S GOING TO ANSWER?', you'd think there was nobody home

ORACLE   Doorbell. It's the Neighbour.

COSMETICS   What neighbour?

ORACLE   The next-door Neighbour.

COSMETICS	Céline's Mother didn't know Céline and René had neighbours. She looks out of the colossal window, the window where you see the colossal avenue of palm trees. She sees a black woman outside the front door
ORACLE	She knocks on the door with her fist.
COSMETICS	Céline's Mother didn't know there were blacks in that neighbourhood. The Mother decides to answer even so. She practises: 'What can I do for you? What can I do for you?', she opens the door – realises she still has the dirty plate in her hand – too late – she's already opening the door. She hides the dirty plate behind her back.
ORACLE	The Neighbour says: 'Good morning. I'm the Neighbour.'
COSMETICS	Maybe not black after all, maybe it's seeing her against the light – her face in the shadow
ORACLE	The Neighbour says: 'Is Isabelle there?'
COSMETICS	Who?
ORACLE	Isabelle.
COSMETICS	The Mother says: 'Does she work here?'
ORACLE	The Neighbour says: 'I know she's there, I can hear music.'
COSMETICS	The Mother says: 'Sorry, I can't help you', and the Mother slowly closes the door

ORACLE   The Neighbour looks her in the eye.

ORACLE *looks at* COSMETICS
SALESPERSON.

COSMETICS   The Mother feels the Neighbour's eyes –
goes on shutting the door. The
Neighbour keeps staring at her, holding
the door back with her gaze, stopping her
shutting it with her eyes – WHAT EYES.
The Neighbour steps forward, her face
comes out of the shadow and her
eyeballs come out of their sockets,
swivelling in all directions – quivering at
the end of their optic nerves. 'Are you
going to close or not, BLOODY
DOOR!' Pushes as hard as she can

ORACLE *looks at the audience.*

The door shuts, clicks, locks – lock the
door, put the security chain on, go back
to the kitchen. But when the Mother sees
her husband at the table from behind, in
his vest, hair on his neck, elbow lifted,
head tilted back – like this – drinking a
beer, a cigarette in his other hand, when
she sees the ash on the floor, the plate –
the dirty plate she had in her hand,
which she's still holding – slips out of her
fingers, and breaks on the dirty kitchen's
dirty floor.

MANAGER   WHAT ARE YOU LOOKING AT ME
FOR? PICK IT UP.

COSMETICS   The Mother doesn't pick it up, she's
running to the bedroom, the floor creaks

under her feet – hand on the doorknob,
ear to the door: no more music. The
Mother goes into – her daughter's
bedroom. She can't see her, it's dark, but
she can hear her breathing. The Mother
goes to the window and opens the
curtains. Outside it's snowing – in the
desert. The Mother closes the curtains,
her eyes get used to the gloom, she can
make out her daughter – her body on the
bed. She's asleep. The Mother thinks: 'I
haven't kissed my daughter yet,' she goes
nearer, she's bending over her – wanting
to kiss her, but her daughter has her eyes
wide open – she's dribbling saliva, her
mouth is stuck to the pillow. Why isn't
she asleep? The Mother's annoyed, her
daughter needs her rest. She certainly
shouldn't be sleeping on her stomach.
She turns her onto her back

ORACLE   And does up her ankles again to the bars
              of the bed.

COSMETICS   In the kitchen

MANAGER   YOU GOING TO PICK UP THE
              FUCKING PLATE?

COSMETICS   The Mother doesn't answer. Goes to the
              sink, gets another plate

MANAGER   NOT THAT ONE, FUCKING
              STUPID! THE ONE YOU BUST.

COSMETICS   ARE YOU HUNGRY?

MANAGER   The Father doesn't answer.

COSMETICS YOU EATEN?

MANAGER WHAT AM I SUPPOSED TO EAT?
YOUR FUCKING

COSMETICS She doesn't give him time to talk about
her fucking pizza, the Mother chucks the
plate at his head – frisbee. He ducks, the
plate gets stuck in the wall – crack! – just
above his head. The plate doesn't break,
because it's not a plate, it's a saucepan
lid. He gets up

MANAGER The Father gets up, the chair falls over:
WHAT'S YOUR FUCKING
PROBLEM?

COSMETICS No time to escape, she's already got hold
of the broom. No time to protect himself
– smack! – breaks the broom on his head,
I mean the broom doesn't break

MANAGER The Father falls on the ground, his hand
on his forehead: CRAZY CUNT

COSMETICS STILL HUNGRY? She keeps hitting him,
short little blows, but hard. He's crying

MANAGER Not crying. WHAT'S THE FUCKING
MATTER WITH YOU?

COSMETICS He's bleeding on the ripped vinyl –
perfect. The broom – the Mother puts
the end of the handle under his nose. He
doesn't move

MANAGER He doesn't move, the kitchen light's
swinging – the Mother's shadow on the
cupboards – gigantic

COSMETICS	WHO WAS THE LAST ONE IN THE BEDROOM?
MANAGER	HOW AM I SUPPOSED TO
COSMETICS	YOU WAS IN THE KITCHEN COULDN'T YOU HEAR?
MANAGER	DIDN'T HEAR NOTHING
COSMETICS	YOU HEARD NOTHING THAT'S BECAUSE IT WAS YOU!
MANAGER	WHAT YOU TRYING TO SAY?
COSMETICS	SHE'S SICK, FOR FUCK'S SAKE! HADN'T YOU NOTICED? SHE MUST NOT GET UP
MANAGER	I DIDN'T MOVE HER
COSMETICS	RIGHT, YOU WANT TO TELL ME WHAT SHE'S DOING ON HER STOMACH?
DISPLAY	The Brother comes into the kitchen – he keeps out of the way
MANAGER	GET YOUR ARSE OVER HERE, YOU CUNT
DISPLAY	He doesn't move
MANAGER	YOU BEEN BACK IN THE BEDROOM?
DISPLAY	WHEN?
MANAGER	DON'T MEAN YESTERDAY DO I
DISPLAY	The Brother backs off

COSMETICS   The Mother goes after him. IT'S YOU
             WHAT UNDID HER?

DISPLAY   I DIDN'T TOUCH HER

COSMETICS   YOU'D BETTER FUCKING NOT
             HAVE OR IT'S YOU GOING TAKE
             HER TO HOSPITAL

MANAGER   The Mother has her back turned. The
             Father seizes his chance – gets up, grabs
             the broom

COSMETICS   DROP THAT

MANAGER   YOU DROP THAT. Snatches the broom
             from her, pushes her with his foot – falls
             on her arse – big arse. Wonderful

COSMETICS   The Mother looks at him. GO ON! HIT
             ME! WHILE YOU GOT THE
             CHANCE

DISPLAY   The broom's in the air, the Father yells

MANAGER   He hits the fridge – twice, the broom
             doesn't break. SHIT

COSMETICS   He tries to break the broom on his knee
             – SISSY! doesn't even crack

DISPLAY   He rests the broom on the worktop and
             tries to break it with his foot, but the
             broom slips

MANAGER   FOR CHRIST'S SAKE! The Father
             drops the broom – picks up a chair

COSMETICS   He lifts up the chair, catches the lightbulb
             on the ceiling – his shadow on the floor

MANAGER   He throws the chair against the wall

DISPLAY   The chair bounces off, falls upright,
                 doesn't break – Ikea

COSMETICS   She starts laughing

DISPLAY   Unbelievable

MANAGER   The Father grabs the Mother by her hair
                 and drags her to the broken plate

COSMETICS   A little bit of the plate gets stuck in her
                 hand. She yells

MANAGER   The Father rubs her face in the pieces. I
                 SAID PICK IT UP! She's wailing

COSMETICS   Not wailing. She's struggling.

DISPLAY   The Brother jumps on the Father

MANAGER   On his back. The Father swings round
                 and smashes the Brother against the fridge

COSMETICS   THE FRIDGE! All the magnets fall off

MANAGER   The Father takes a swing at him

DISPLAY   Smashes the Brother to the ground

MANAGER   The Father gets him in a hold – the vice.
                 The Brother's head between his knees
                 and he squeezes

DISPLAY   The Father finds this funny

MANAGER   Because he's seeing his head upside down
                 – his mouth upside down. It's like a
                 goblin face. His hair's a beard. His chin's
                 a pointy head

DISPLAY   The Brother's shouting

MANAGER   With creases for a mouth and a mouth in
               his forehead

COSMETICS   A long dribble of slobber

DISPLAY   Father spits in the Brother's mouth

MANAGER   The Brother's choking – wailing

DISPLAY   Not wailing, catching his breath – he gets
               free

MANAGER   No, it's the Father lets him go.

COSMETICS   The three of them, sitting in the kitchen
               – not a word – breathing. Clang! The
               saucepan lid comes away from the wall
               – out of the crack, falls on the floor,
               rolls

DISPLAY   The lid rolls clear of the wall, the chair.
               It makes smaller and smaller circles,
               turning on itself faster and faster – trrr! –
               and it stops.

COSMETICS   She gets up and picks it up

MANAGER   Gets up and goes for a piss

DISPLAY   Gets up, TV – Nintendo – Super Mario

COSMETICS   Kitchen – living room. She watches her
               son playing. He's good. YOU GET
               SOME?

DISPLAY   Pause – Mario's hovering. Gives her the
               bag

COSMETICS   THE CARD

DISPLAY	Gives her the credit card. Mario falls over and kicks the tortoise
COSMETICS	Empties the bag on the table, makes four lines with the card, rolls up a ten, sniffs a line
MANAGER	In the living room – mobile, beer, cold pizza. The Father's got the box on his lap, throwing crusts at the Brother
DISPLAY	FOR CHRIST'S SAKE. Level three – ice slides.
MANAGER	GOT SOME MAGAZINES?
DISPLAY	NOTHING ABOUT CÉLINE.
MANAGER	CAMERA?
DISPLAY	I GOT ONE THROWAWAY LEFT. Lost concentration – loses a life
COSMETICS	GIVE ME THAT. Mario's sliding, surfing – it's all turns. The handset's clicking. OKAY! The Mother's never got that far before – pause. Another line, scrape – gulp it down. Unpause, continue
MANAGER	BONUS. She never takes her bonus
DISPLAY	SECRET PASSAGE
COSMETICS	SHUT YOUR FACES! Mario breaks off his glide, skate-skate, steams ahead, back on his tracks – one hundred and eighty – up against the wall of ice
DISPLAY	Sees himself in it and goes right through

MANAGER   Light through the window. Their
             shadows are stretching, writhing

DISPLAY   Running through the room, over the
             walls – turning round

MANAGER   The snowplough crosses the desert of –
             of the empty parking lot.

ORACLE   Close your eyes.

             MANAGER, COSMETICS
             SALESPERSON *and* DISPLAY
             ASSISTANT *close their eyes.*

             Now, imagine what sort of life you'd have
             had if you'd always been in bed. Imagine
             the life of Isabelle, Céline's fan, lying in
             her bedroom, her sick girl's bedroom,
             curtains always drawn – light years away
             from her idol's bedroom in Las Vegas.
             Imagine yellowing paint, carpet coming
             unstuck, dusty curtains, imagine the chest
             of drawers, the broken mirror, the plastic
             flowers to give some colour. Imagine the
             posters, photos, articles about Céline
             which decorate the walls, and stuck
             against one wall, pushed into a corner,
             Isabelle's bed, which is too small but
             takes up all the room in the bedroom.
             Imagine Isabelle, lying on her mattress,
             dreaming of Céline, because all she can
             do to fight her illness is dream of Céline.
             Céline is her only hope, even though
             Isabelle's not going to get better. Isabelle's
             in the last stage of her illness. The only
             thing keeping her alive is Céline –

photos, articles, songs by Céline. Céline is her whole life and in her life everything is Céline. Isabelle is a fan of Céline, but without Céline Isabelle wouldn't be a fan, so she'd be nothing. She'd just be a body without a name. If I said: 'Céline's dead' Isabelle would begin to decompose, or better still if I said: 'Céline's like Father Christmas, she's not really true,' then Isabelle would – burst, spatter over the walls – explode, and when you've imagined all that, when you've managed to feel the smell of the room, the broken springs of the mattress – stained mattress, no covers for Isabelle, when the springs are starting to make you feel ill, you put your fingers inside yourself

COSMETICS   Isabelle's Mother opens her eyes: WHAT? The blue of the TV, the line of coke – hears a noise, goes out of the living room, goes into the bedroom. Her daughter – sweating, having a fit. IT'S STARTING AGAIN!

MANAGER   The Father opens his eyes: the blue of the TV

COSMETICS   Shouldn't have just tied up her feet

DISPLAY   The Brother hears the Mother calling

COSMETICS   COME AND HELP. She's been playing in it – her hands all bloody

MANAGER   The Father comes into the bedroom. His daughter's crying but without crying, mouth open – eyes scrunched up

COSMETICS HOLD HER

DISPLAY   The Brother comes into the bedroom

MANAGER   Her Father gets hold of her wrists – from
           behind, because she's trying to bite him.
           He holds her wrists with one hand, gets
           her chin with the other, she bites his
           finger SHIT

COSMETICS DON'T SWEAR! She's struggling

MANAGER   PUT ON A CD

DISPLAY   The Brother runs to the CDs, in the dark
           – bumps into the chest of drawers

COSMETICS PHOTOS OF CÉLINE FIRST

DISPLAY   On the chest of drawers – picks up the
           throwaway camera

COSMETICS WHERE THEY GONE?

MANAGER   LOOK UNDERNEATH. She's trying to
           lick him

COSMETICS Picks up an old magazine from under the
           bed, opens it to the centre page:
           'CÉLINE AND RENÉ HAVE A LIE-
           IN'

DISPLAY   Looks for a good angle – too dark

MANAGER   LOOK. She doesn't want to – shakes her
           head

COSMETICS Turns the page

DISPLAY   Click – turns on the flash

COSMETICS   Reads the caption: 'CÉLINE'S
             LOOKING FOR A NAME FOR HER
             BABY.'

MANAGER   Opens her eyes with his fingers

DISPLAY   The flash goes off by itself

COSMETICS   'I WANT MY CHILD TO KNOW
             HOW MUCH HE WAS LOOKED
             FORWARD TO, WANTED'

DISPLAY   She focuses

COSMETICS   'HOW MUCH HIS FATHER LOVED
             HIS MOTHER AND HIS MOTHER
             LOVED HIS FATHER'

MANAGER   Her arms relax

COSMETICS   'HOW MUCH THE WHOLE FAMILY
             LOVED EACH OTHER AND WERE
             LOOKING FORWARD TO HIS
             ARRIVAL.'

MANAGER   LOOK. She stares at the picture and
             smiles. The Father can let go of her wrists

COSMETICS   The Mother signals to the Brother to
             come closer. 'I AM A FULFILLED
             WOMAN.'

MANAGER   She straightens herself up, getting into
             the same pose as in the magazine

COSMETICS   'CÉLINE WEARS CHANEL.'

DISPLAY   The Brother puts his eye to the
             viewfinder

ORACLE   He sees his Father from behind – his
              back completely covered with hair

MANAGER   TAKE A PICTURE. QUICK

DISPLAY   Click! The flash goes off

ORACLE   Her mother has her eyes half-closed,
              caught with something like the beginning
              of a smile

MANAGER   TAKE ANOTHER

DISPLAY   Click –

COSMETICS   'CÉLINE HAS FILM PROJECTS.'

ORACLE   You'd think she was reading her a
              bedtime story – to send her to sleep

DISPLAY   Click!

ORACLE   What's odd isn't her smile. It's the fact
              that her Mother's breasts are bare.

COSMETICS   The Mother moves back

DISPLAY   The flash goes off

ORACLE   From the position of his arm, you can tell
              the Father's just taking off his belt.

MANAGER   The Father gets up

COSMETICS   PUT ON A CD

ORACLE   You never see the Brother. He's taking
              the pictures.

DISPLAY   The Brother turns round. I'M GOING
              TO PUT A CD ON

ORACLE   You can't see her very well. Her face is
                blurred

COSMETICS PRESS 'PLAY'

ORACLE   The white marks either side of the bed
                are her feet

MANAGER   'PLAY' – PRESS 'PLAY'

ORACLE   You can't see her eyes – her mouth is like
                a dark stain

COSMETICS ARE YOU PLAYING IT OR WHAT?

ORACLE   That's how you can tell she has her eyes
                shut and she's crying, mouth open – eyes
                screwed up

MANAGER/
COSMETICS/
DISPLAY   'PLAY'!

                *The song 'Partout Je Te Vois (I See You
                Everywhere)' bursts out. MANAGER,
                COSMETICS SALESPERSON,
                DISPLAY ASSISTANT are all crying,
                mouths open, eyes screwed up.*

ORACLE   Go on.

COSMETICS The skin on her back

DISPLAY   Her cheeks – . Her wrists, big as this

MANAGER   Her belly swollen up like a balloon

DISPLAY   Like a pregnant woman, or rather

MANAGER   No. Malnutrition or

COSMETICS   She could hardly walk

DISPLAY   She couldn't walk. They dragged her

COSMETICS   The Receptionist had seen plenty of
                      rubbish people specially since she moved
                      to Sherbrooke. But this – that one, with
                      her – dress

DISPLAY   'A skeleton,' thought the Security Guard

COSMETICS   At the desk – war. Her Mother said she
                      had indigestion 'again'. Her Father said
                      she was faking – he was smiling

MANAGER   How could her Father smile?

COSMETICS   It was clear she hadn't eaten for a long
                      time or been washed. They brought her
                      to hospital because they 'couldn't stand
                      her any more'.

DISPLAY   You'd think her parents resented her
                      being ill.

COSMETICS   The Receptionist told them to go and sit
                      down. She heard the Mother say: 'Happy
                      now? Star of the show?'

DISPLAY   Unbelievable

MANAGER   Not a word from her. She was looking
                      straight ahead – into space

DISPLAY   Her Brother was taking photos in the
                      waiting room – with a throwaway camera

COSMETICS   The Receptionist couldn't hear herself
                      think

DISPLAY   You couldn't hear anything except the
               irritating little sound of the throwaway
               camera which the Brother kept clicking
               and clicking. A family of lunatics

MANAGER   When the Doctor called her name, they
               didn't get up – no one reacted at all, not
               even Isabelle

COSMETICS   The Nurse had to

MANAGER   Not the Nurse, the Receptionist

COSMETICS   The Nurse who was ALSO doing
               reception –

ORACLE   The Nurse-Receptionist

COSMETICS   The Nurse-Receptionist had to go and
               find them – took Isabelle's arm but they
               didn't want to let go of her

DISPLAY   They didn't want to let her go

MANAGER   They didn't want her to be examined all
               by herself. The Doctor shut his eyes as if
               to stop himself from

DISPLAY   The Security Guard had to threaten
               them – the only language people like that
               understand.

MANAGER   Isabelle's body on the examination table
               – a stain on the white paper. The Doctor
               didn't even examine her

COSMETICS   I mean you only had to look at her:
               suffering, violence, poverty

MANAGER   The Doctor went straightaway to tell the
           parents he was keeping her in – they
           could go home

COSMETICS The Mother was angry as if she thought
           someone was playing a trick on her

MANAGER   The Father: 'What's she doing that to us
           for?'

DISPLAY   The Brother was crying – the Security
           Guard had confiscated his camera. He'd
           'see it tomorrow' if he was good

COSMETICS The Nurse-Receptionist checked with the
           Father that she had the right telephone
           number – his mobile, so she could reach
           them in an emergency, knowing perfectly
           well she wouldn't call them even in an
           emergency. 'The last people to call in an
           emergency,' thought the Nurse-Receptionist

DISPLAY   The Security Guard ordered them to go
           home.

MANAGER   During the examination, the Doctor
           asked Isabelle where she'd got the
           bruises, if something had happened – an
           accident. She didn't say anything – she
           didn't answer, as if she didn't understand.
           The infection was advanced. Isabelle's
           belly was hard and purple. You could see
           huge veins running under her skin.
           Dropsy? Neurofibrositis?

COSMETICS Probably the result of a home abortion –
           which she'd done to herself or – more
           likely

MANAGER   But the Doctor didn't mention abortion
             to Isabelle. He'd wait for the results – till
             she saw the Psychiatrist.

COSMETICS   In the bath, Isabelle hid her sex with her
             hands – protecting herself. Rubbing her
             back, the Nurse thought: 'Indigestion
             doesn't make your ankles bleed.' Isabelle
             didn't want to eat or drink anything, or
             open her mouth. The Nurse gave her
             medicine intravenously

DISPLAY   When the Security Guard came into the
             room, Isabelle was asleep. He put the
             throwaway camera on the bedside table,
             next to the mirror and the flowers –
             where you couldn't miss it.

COSMETICS   Isabelle slept for twelve hours. The Nurse
             had made sure to shut the curtains. Next
             day, the Nurse came in pushing her trolley
             slowly without making a sound. When she
             opened the curtains, Isabelle was already
             up – I mean her eyes were wide open.
             The Nurse asked her if she'd / slept well

ORACLE   The Nurse-Receptionist stops speaking
             when she sees Isabelle.

COSMETICS   Why?

ORACLE   Her belly

COSMETICS   What about her belly?

ORACLE   Isabelle's belly's got bigger.

DISPLAY   The Psychiatrist comes into the room.
             When he sees Isabelle's belly, he can't

                              understand why the Nurse-Receptionist
                              isn't already running out – to call the
                              Doctor

COSMETICS   She DOESN'T WANT to frighten her.
             She's not crying – doesn't seem to be in
             pain. The Nurse-Receptionist gives the
             Psychiatrist a meaningful look and goes
             out calmly

DISPLAY   The Psychiatrist puts the table over the
             bed, even though it's not his job. He says:
             'Good morning,' as if nothing was
             wrong. Isabelle doesn't reply – nothing at
             all. He puts the tray on the table and
             puts a pillow behind her back. Isabelle
             lets him do it and does nothing herself –
             she smiles. Nervous shock?
             Schizophrenia? The Psychiatrist picks up
             the teaspoon and the fruit salad

ORACLE   Isabelle takes the Psychiatrist's pen out of
             his shirt pocket.

DISPLAY   The Psychiatrist is pleased. Isabelle's
             trying in her own way to make contact –
             she wants to play

ORACLE   She wants to write.

DISPLAY   The Psychiatrist takes a piece of paper –
             his pad – and gives it to her

ORACLE   Isabelle's writing.

DISPLAY   What?

ORACLE   A letter.

DISPLAY   What does she say in her letter?

ORACLE   The Psychiatrist doesn't have time to
               read it, the Nurse comes from behind
               and takes the letter

COSMETICS   The Nurse takes the letter and reads it

ORACLE   Not the Nurse

COSMETICS   The Nurse-RECEPTIONIST

ORACLE   Not her, a different one. The Night Nurse

DISPLAY   / What's that?

MANAGER   Since when?

               ORACLE *looks at* DISPLAY
               ASSISTANT.

ORACLE   The Psychiatrist sees the Night Nurse's
               hand taking the letter, he sees her night
               arm

DISPLAY   The Psychiatrist shuts his eyes

ORACLE   His eyes can't shut, his eyes can still just
               see, they go up the Nurse's arm

DISPLAY   Turns his head

ORACLE   Can't – sees her uniform

DISPLAY   Doesn't look

ORACLE   LOOKS at the nametag on the uniform,
               the name, the BACKWARDS
               LETTERS

DISPLAY   DOESN'T LOOK

ORACLE	TOO LATE. The Psychiatrist has to read my name: ORACLE. He has to see my eyes, which are looking at him, looking right into his eyes. I'm moving away, making off with the letter, sliding like a shadow – towards the mirror. I take the hospital flowers – the plastic flowers – take the throwaway camera. I stop in front of the mirror. I'm looking at you. You're looking at me. We smile at each other – disappear.

ORACLE *faces the audience.*

MANAGER	The Doctor comes into the room
COSMETICS	The Nurse-Receptionist comes into the room
MANAGER	The Doctor freezes
DISPLAY	The Psychiatrist can't move – his eyes are riveted to the mirror
COSMETICS	The Nurse puts a hand to her mouth
DISPLAY	The Psychiatrist sees their reflections, frozen. He turns – at last he can turn – slowly turns his head towards Isabelle
MANAGER	The Doctor goes up to the bed
COSMETICS	The Nurse behind him
MANAGER	Isabelle's belly is enormous
COSMETICS	You'd think – it was swelling up
MANAGER	The Doctor's seen the X-rays. The dropsy was concealing a cancer – an

enormous tumour. The Doctor has in his head a negative of a tumour getting bigger – while you look at it

COSMETICS   Isabelle isn't crying – I mean she doesn't seem to be in pain

MANAGER   Isabelle's smiling. She gives a pen to the Psychiatrist

DISPLAY   The Psychiatrist takes his pen back

MANAGER   The Doctor puts his hand on Isabelle's belly – delicately. He says: 'How are you feeling today?'

ORACLE   And then you say: 'I feel good. Always do.'

DISPLAY   But Isabelle's lips don't move – they stay closed.

COSMETICS   Who says: 'I feel good. Always do'?

MANAGER   The Doctor doesn't use his stethoscope, he puts his ear directly on Isabelle's belly

ORACLE   The Doctor hears: 'Me.'

MANAGER   The voice – the voice is coming from inside her belly

ORACLE   And then you say: 'I'm called Caro. I'm the biggest fan.'

MANAGER   The Doctor slowly lifts Isabelle's pyjama jacket

COSMETICS   The belly – inside – completely black

DISPLAY   The Psychiatrist can't look

MANAGER   Swollen – black liquid

DISPLAY   But his eyes keep trying to find, trying
despite himself, are FORCED TO TRY
AND FIND. Between her thighs, there's
something missing – sex, anus

ORACLE   Isabelle's got no hole, no crack. No way
out except her mouth because
everything's coming out of her mouth,
which is opening after all. Isabelle can,
after all. She can after all speak, she wants
to speak – too late. Her air's cut off, her
vocal cords are blocked, her mouth's
filling up, overflowing, opening with a
river of black bile which bursts out
horizontally and falls, splattering the
white sheets. Isabelle's vomiting,
completely, endlessly emptying her belly.
The bile overflows and runs onto the
white floor and spreads through the
hospital room. The Doctor, the Nurse
and the Psychiatrist skate towards the
door, fall over, get up, fall over again,
howling and burning. They melt, turn
black and disappear under the
overwhelming wave of sick. Isabelle
vomits till she's empty, on and on, her
mouth open, her eyes popping out, her
navel touching her spine. Inside her,
something's turning inside out – like a
glove. Something's coming up and out
and on and on: a long scarf of joined-up
handkerchiefs – like a conjuring trick.
Liver, kidneys, stomach, intestines –
dedaah! – with her lungs, which are

collapsing, and her heart, which is
fluttering, on the end. Hanging out of her
mouth: her oesophagus, which has come
out backwards. She takes her oesophagus
in her fingers and instinctively wants to
pull, but she tells herself: 'Swallow,
swallow.' She wants to swallow her heart,
she gets hold of her heart and opens her
mouth, but her shoulder comes adrift and
all the rest follows. Her left arm's turning
back on itself as she vomits it out. The
bones are breaking away from the muscles
and they fall – a little white heap at her
feet – till her arm's hanging from her
mouth, empty, inside out. She goes up to
the mirror and looks at the inside of her
arm, the veins and nerves, like the finger
of a big red plastic glove turned inside
out. Flush! Someone's flushed the toilet
but she doesn't wonder who's there, she's
just trying to swallow her left arm before
anyone comes. 'Swallow, swallow,' but she
vomits her right arm, which empties itself
and turns inside out, followed by her left
leg – she falls on the floor – and her right
leg – slides on her back. On her back with
four tubes of meat coming out of her
mouth, she thinks: 'God, I must look so
silly' and vomits her ribcage and spine,
which knock out her teeth and jaw on the
way through. With a pop! her skull bursts
– grey matter's running down like wet
cement. Her head turns inside out – a
floppy wig, and comes out backwards
through her mouth and once she's spat

out the pieces of skull she can vomit her pelvis and the rest of the spine down to the coccyx, which comes out of her mouth, and her mouth turns inside out and vomits itself. You're not wondering how anyone can live without a skeleton, you're just wondering if anyone's seen you, and you find a way of holding yourself up on your floppy inside-out legs and of finding your optic nerves in the folds of your inside-out face with your floppy inside-out hands and pulling on them so you can get your eyes out. Even if your eyeballs are swivelling in all directions, you can see the white of the sink, the tap, the running water. Take your fingers out of your mouth, lift your head, look in the mirror. You can see your nametag in the mirror, read the letters of your name, preceded by your employee number: 31CARO. Backwards that says: ORACLE. I'm looking at you. You're looking at me. We smile at each other. Quick, Caro. Hide the plastic flowers in your backpack.

COSMETICS   I come out of the toilet.

ORACLE   In the mirror you see the Cosmetics Salesperson come out of the toilet.

COSMETICS   I look at Caro: poor little cow.

ORACLE   Dry your mouth, turn off the tap.

COSMETICS   I go up to her – to the next sink. I say: 'Not feeling better?'

ORACLE   Through the tannoy on the ceiling:
            Céline, hard to make out.

COSMETICS   I turn on the tap for no reason – wash
            my hands. I see her bag down by her
            feet. I say: 'What are you doing after
            work?' Imagine an evening with Caro:
            death.

ORACLE   You're about to say: 'I'm going to listen
            to Céline's latest DVD,' but you don't
            have time, the music breaks off right in
            the middle of the chorus. '31 to checkout
            number 8.' You dry your hands on your
            overalls though there is a hand-drier, but
            the Cosmetics Salesperson's using the
            hand-drier

COSMETICS   The hot air isn't very hot, I'm rubbing
            my hands hard – I watch her go out. I
            say: 'Come and eat with us at lunch' –
            out of guilt.

ORACLE   Open the door – the chorus is drowned
            out by the noise of the store. Go and put
            your bag in the staffroom, go down the
            corridor, come out onto the floor: section
            7, 'Men's Underwear'. Céline is playing a
            bit louder. The Display Assistant's talking
            to the new girl, pretending not to see you.
            He's thinking of something to say to
            make her laugh. The new girl laughs
            anyway, maybe because she saw a bit of
            intestine sticking out under your overall

DISPLAY   Caro goes by, doing up her overall. I
            pretend not to see her – pick a piece of

paper up off the floor even though it's not my job. Unbelievable. She spends her whole time in the toilet – her whole break.

ORACLE 'The hardest thing about work is other people – hearing what they think.' You wonder if there's a kind of work where people are all alone – really all alone. Lighthousekeeper. Section 12, 'Boots and Shoes', the words of the song 'I See You Everywhere' are loud and clear. A salesman whistles the tune while he gets a pair of shoes ready – takes off the paper. Watch out, at the end of 13: the Manager's looking at you with his arms folded

MANAGER There are two kinds of employees: the ones who work and the ones who pretend to work – simple as that.

ORACLE You bend your head – hurry, but it's hard to hurry when your legs are floppy and inside out.

MANAGER I stare at her without saying anything. Always works.

ORACLE The cashier at checkout number 7 still has the phone in her hand – wiping it, and hangs up. The click cuts into the song while Céline's holding the note at the end. Go to your checkout, take off the 'CHECKOUT CLOSED' sign, and wait. The cashier at checkout number 7 sighs and says: 'Move along to the next checkout, please,' almost crying. The customers did understand, they were just trying to work out if it's worth changing queues and risking losing their place.

MANAGER   Basically there are two kinds of employees: the ones who steal and the ones who don't steal.

ORACLE   The second-to-last person in the queue finally makes a move – too late, the last one's quicker. He throws himself at your checkout – gets in front. You say: 'Do you have your Wal-Mart card?', telling him off.

MANAGER   I watch 31 talking to her customer: doesn't smile enough.

ORACLE   Credit card – doesn't work: wrong PIN number. The customer's head's somewhere else – not concentrating.

MANAGER   I go behind checkout 8. Her shoes comply with regulations.

ORACLE   The customer who was pushed out the way puts down his blender. He takes a Céline DVD off the rack – a look and a smile.

MANAGER   The customer pays cash.

ORACLE   You say: 'Thank you, have a nice day.'

MANAGER   'Have a nice day and thank you for shopping at Wal-Mart,' but I don't take 31 up on it. I say: 'Caro, come and see me in my office. When you have a moment.' Meaning: 'At the beginning of your lunch hour.'

DISPLAY   I'm going towards the checkouts and I
                 see the Manager standing behind Caro:
                 endless training.

MANAGER   I see the Display Assistant looking for
                 something to do. I go back to the centre
                 aisle and walk to 21, 'Toy Section'.

DISPLAY   I catch up with the Manager and walk
                 behind him – almost running. I'm
                 waiting for orders.

ORACLE   Section 21 swallows them up. The centre
                 aisle is empty. You've no customers at
                 your checkout. You look at number 7.
                 She's got her back to you, she's talking to
                 number 6, 5's talking to 4, 3 to 2, who's 1
                 talking to? No time to talk to anyone,
                 she's always busy, it's the checkout for
                 'Two articles or less'. A night job.
                 Security Guard – at the shopping centre.
                 You'd be really alone there. You'd walk
                 down the corridors. There'd be no one to
                 see you. The shop-window dummies
                 wouldn't frighten you. You'd say on your
                 radio: 'Checking at Wal-Mart.' You'd
                 take out your keys, you'd open the
                 revolving doors, and once you were
                 inside you'd take off your cap and your
                 uniform. You wouldn't need to hide in
                 the toilet any more. You'd walk through
                 all the sections completely naked. You'd
                 get yourself some flowers from 17,
                 'Interior Decoration'. You'd go up the
                 escalator to the second floor. You'd
                 choose a bed in a demonstration room

with a mirror and a chest of drawers.
You'd put on a DVD – never the same
one. One night it'd be the concert at the
Stade de France, another time it'd be – .
A customer appears in front of you and
makes you jump. She says: 'Hello, lovely,'
but without looking at you. She
rummages in her handbag with her head
down. You can't see her eyes because
she's wearing dark glasses. You look for
her purchases – can't see any, what did
she buy? But then you spot the bottle of
perfume – something expensive – the
perfume called Céline Perfume. You pick
up the bottle of perfume, beep! it goes
through, you're about to tell her the price
but the right money's already on the
counter and the whole meaning of the
song 'Incognito' is suddenly revealed to
you. You don't have to look, you know it's
her. She puts one hand on your inside-
out hand and there's just her and you in
an empty silent Wal-Mart. She says: 'I've
been looking for you for a long time', and
you're crying and you can't stop. You
push the money gently back towards her
and she understands that this is the
moment when you can give her back all
the love she's given you. Between sobs
you say: 'I'm your biggest fan.' She looks
at you then with your eyes starting out of
your head and your eyeballs swivelling
round and she smiles. She loves you, ugly
as you are. She picks up a *Live in Las Vegas*
DVD from the checkout rack and takes

out a pen and signs it. She gives you the
DVD and puts the money in her purse,
the bottle of perfume in her handbag,
saying: 'Thank you,' but without saying
thank you, just mouthing the words
'Thank you', and she goes and meets her
Bodyguard at the Wal-Mart entrance –
and disappears. On the DVD she's
written 'Céline' diagonally and just above
it 'See you soon.' Number 7 asks what's
so funny, taking an interest for once, but
you go: 'You wouldn't understand' and
wipe away a tear. It's time. Hide the
DVD, close your checkout, put up the
sign 'CHECKOUT CLOSED' and walk
down the centre aisle without hurrying.
Our secret.

MANAGER   She comes into my office without
knocking – and smiling.

ORACLE   You know what the Manager's going to
say: your shoes don't comply with
regulations. But he doesn't know what it's
like living without a skeleton.

MANAGER   She sits down without being told.

ORACLE   But when he learns that Céline in person
came to your checkout

MANAGER   I'm waiting for her to realise.

ORACLE   He'll understand – he'll understand why
you didn't make her pay for the bottle of
perfume. He'll congratulate you even.

MANAGER   She's just realised.

ORACLE   What's your bag doing on the Manager's
            desk?

MANAGER   I say: 'Open it.'

ORACLE   Don't open it.

MANAGER   And I say: 'There are things I can
            understand and things I can't
            understand. If an employee doesn't feel
            good and it affects their work to a certain
            extent, I can understand that. But if an
            employee who doesn't feel good and
            whose work is GREATLY affected by
            their state of mind then goes on to steal,
            that I can't understand.'

ORACLE   In your bag: your lunch, and the plastic
            flowers with their label.

MANAGER   'I don't understand and I don't want to
            understand.' No pity. I stare at the plastic
            flowers.

ORACLE   How could he understand?

MANAGER   How can she smile?

ORACLE   Céline understands you. She looked for
            you. She found you. She wrote: 'See you
            soon.' She's waiting for you. You have the
            DVD to prove it – NO – don't show it to
            him. Say nothing about it – our secret.
            Pick up your bag

MANAGER   I pick up something on my desk – an
            order form. 'You're not coming back
            tomorrow.'

ORACLE   Get up, put on your backpack, go out of
            the Manager's office – out of the office,
            back through section 7, 'Men's
            Underwear', into the corridor, past the
            toilets. Into the staffroom. The Display
            Assistant is sitting at the table reading the
            paper. The Cosmetics Salesperson is
            waiting by the microwave. Put your bag
            on the rack

COSMETICS   I saw her do it – put the flowers in her
            backpack.

ORACLE   Take out your lunch

DISPLAY   I look up: Caro.

ORACLE   Act just like it's lunch break

COSMETICS   Personally I don't give a fuck.

ORACLE   Act like nothing's wrong

COSMETICS   Plastic flowers, not a big deal.

DISPLAY   Not eating her lunch in the toilets?
            Something must have happened.

COSMETICS   I could have kept my big mouth shut.

ORACLE   Like an ordinary day.

COSMETICS   But the truth is I can't stand her – the
            sight of her.

ORACLE   Even if Céline did appear at your
            checkout the day her latest DVD's come
            out, don't say anything – our secret, just
            the two of us. It would make them
            miserable – they'd be jealous

DISPLAY   'Caro' isn't short for Caroline. Her
                 parents really called her that, just 'Caro'.

COSMETICS   There's something – dead about her eyes.

ORACLE   Hide the album signed 'See you soon –
                 Céline' at the bottom of your bag

DISPLAY   One look at her and I feel sick. With her
                 half-name.

ORACLE   Take your lunch, turn round, look the
                 Cosmetics Salesperson right in the eye

COSMETICS   I say: 'Welcome to our humble abode!'
                 That wasn't necessary.

ORACLE   Go and sit opposite the Display Assistant

DISPLAY   I'm still reading the paper, even though I
                 want to shout: 'WHAT HAVE YOU
                 GOT TO SMILE ABOUT, YOU
                 POOR SPASTIC?'

ORACLE   And look. Look at the front page of the
                 paper. At the top you can see a picture of
                 an American actress with her mouth
                 open. In the middle, a picture of an Iraqi
                 father holding his dead son in his arms –
                 and his mouth is open too, but his eyes
                 are scrunched up. You'd think they were
                 two contestants on *Star Academy*

COSMETICS   I wait two seconds after the beep and
                 take my lasagna out of the microwave
                 and go and sit next to her – out of guilt.

DISPLAY   I hate it when someone reads the paper
                 at the same time as me. I turn the page
                 with a flick.

COSMETICS   I say to Caro: 'What did you make yourself for lunch?'

ORACLE   On the second page, you can see a big publicity shot of Céline. 'WIN A TRIP TO LAS VEGAS TO SEE CÉLINE.' You see Céline putting make-up on in front of a mirror in her dressing room

COSMETICS   She doesn't answer – want to hit her.

DISPLAY   I put the paper on the table so she can read it too. I say: 'FUCK.'

COSMETICS   I say: 'What?'

DISPLAY   'FUCK' referring to the article, but it was for Caro – stupid fuck.

ORACLE   The Display Assistant has put the paper on the table. It's hard to read the headline on page three because the words are upside down.

MANAGER   Why didn't I tell her to leave right away? She'll use her last afternoon to steal something else or break something – have her revenge.

ORACLE   ACCUSED is easy enough to make out because of the two Cs

COSMETICS   I say: 'Is it the girl from Sherbrooke who died of cancer of the ovaries?' as if there'd been one who died of lung cancer, one of prostate cancer, one had her leg cut off, and so on.

MANAGER   Not in the toilets – a bad sign.

ORACLE   'ACCUSED OF AGGRESSION' –
           'AGGRESSION' backwards is
           'NOISSERGGA'. That doesn't mean
           anything.

DISPLAY   I say: 'It wasn't just the father, it was the
           whole family.'

COSMETICS I say: 'Let's have a look.'

MANAGER   Not in the children's play area either.

ORACLE   'ORACLE' means something.

DISPLAY   I look at the photo of the victim when
           she was little. Her smile – unbearable.

COSMETICS 'Let's have a look.'

DISPLAY   I give the paper to the Cosmetics
           Salesperson.

ORACLE   You can see it upside down, read the
           headline, see the picture, the picture of
           the Father, who's walking along with his
           head down. The Cosmetics Salesperson
           unfolds the paper but it's a trap. On the
           left-hand page the publicity photo: Céline
           putting on make-up in her dressing room.
           On the right-hand page, the picture of
           the Father outside the court. He's going
           past a little frozen crowd shouting:
           'MONSTER! MURDERER!' He's
           about to go into the courtroom

MANAGER   I go into the staffroom

ORACLE   The courtroom.

MANAGER   What courtroom?

ORACLE   The Father's going into the courtroom –
              the trial

MANAGER   The Father doesn't go in, / he steps back

              ORACLE *looks at* MANAGER.

ORACLE   The Father has to go in, he's under escort

MANAGER   WHAT'VE I DONE? NOT DONE /
              NOTHING

ORACLE   THE MOTHER TALKED

COSMETICS   THE MOTHER DIDN'T SAY
              NOTHING!

              ORACLE *takes the throwaway camera out of
              her overall.*

ORACLE   The jury were horrified by the photos.

              ORACLE *looks at the audience.*

COSMETICS   The Mother told the judge – she didn't
              want a second child

MANAGER   According to the accused, she told the
              landlord: 'THE CHILD BENEFIT'LL
              PAY FOR THE COKE'

COSMETICS   They called her Isabelle, but he called
              her 'SPUNKBAG', accused the Mother

MANAGER   'SHE DIDN'T PUT ANY NAPPIES
              ON HER. SHE LET HER PISS AND
              SHIT ON THE FLOOR,' said the
              victim's Brother

DISPLAY   The Father said to his son: 'LOOK,
              SHE'S A GASH,' while masturbating
              her with a Pepsi bottle

COSMETICS   'HE DIDN'T WANT HER TO GO TO SCHOOL,' said the Mother

MANAGER   'SHE'S THE ONE THOUGHT OF SHACKLES'

DISPLAY   Usually it was the Father, sometimes the Mother. The Brother took photos. He's the one who put on music – CDs of Céline – to drown her cries

COSMETICS   One day, a neighbour saw Isabelle cross in front of her bedroom window

MANAGER   One of the members of the family had forgotten to tie her up

ORACLE   'But how could Isabelle have survived all those years of torture?' asks the newspaper at the end of the article. Easy.

MANAGER   Lunch break's over.

COSMETICS   I close the paper, pick up the plate, open the dishwasher, put the plate in the dishwasher.

DISPLAY   I rub my hands together, get up.

MANAGER   I must tell Caro to leave.

ORACLE   The hardest thing is hearing people think. The hardest thing is seeing what they see. When Isabelle's finished vomiting, she gets up and walks to the mirror. That's difficult. Isabelle has never walked in her life. She drags herself, slips in the bile, leans on the wall. She hangs on to the chest of drawers, gets in front of the mirror – the mirror in the hospital bedroom, and in the mirror Isabelle looks at herself. From then on, everything's easy. Because in the mirror, Isabelle doesn't see herself. Isabelle sees Céline. In the mirror Isabelle just sees Céline – her dressing room – Céline putting on make-up in her dressing room. She can even see the reflection of the camera behind her. The lunch break's over – start again.

MANAGER, COSMETICS SALESPERSON *and* DISPLAY ASSISTANT *smile.*

DISPLAY   The Cameraman steps back, they're bringing the box

COSMETICS   Céline says 'bye-bye' in the mirror – to the camera – and curls up in a little ball in the box

DISPLAY   They close the box and roll it under the stage. The camera can't go under the stage to see what's going on under the stage – with René

MANAGER   Under the stage – 'bring out the tiger in her'

DISPLAY   That's right

MANAGER   René's walking round Céline miming a whip. Céline roars

ORACLE   No

DISPLAY   After that, Céline gets back in the box. The show begins, the box comes up and Céline

ORACLE   NO. That was for the tour. Céline doesn't
              appear out of the floor here. Céline
              comes on from the wings, straight onto
              the stage of / Caesars Palace

COSMETICS   Caesars Palace – YES – microphone in
              her hand and she's going to simply,
              straightforwardly talk to her public. She
              says: 'You can't / imagine

DISPLAY   imagine how happy we are to see you
              here'

COSMETICS   As if we were in her kitchen, in her home,
              with her. 'It's extraordinary, thank you.'

DISPLAY   There – applause. Céline looks down

COSMETICS   'Here we are in this wonderfully
              beautiful, huge, magnificent theatre'

MANAGER   No – not 'huge, magnificent':
              'INCOMPARABLE'

COSMETICS   'Incomparable' – 'We've rehearsed the
              songs and we're feeling inspired. I'm
              surrounded by / wonderful people'

MANAGER   'WONDERFUL.' Yes

DISPLAY   'We've been so longing to do it live,' and
              at that everyone felt they were with her

COSMETICS   Then, to everyone, holding out her hand:
              'I want to thank you for making our
              dream come true. Despite everything
              that's happening'

DISPLAY   Dot dot dot, tears in her eyes, emotional
              pause

COSMETICS   'Let's try to hope / for

MANAGER   There's a sigh after: 'LET'S TRY'

DISPLAY   'LET'S TRY' is said with a sigh

COSMETICS   'Let's try – to hope for peace.'

MANAGER   And then, for the musicians and dancers:
'Let's go, let's have fun!'

DISPLAY   The first bars start to play

ORACLE   And that's when I go into the hospital
bedroom and put the flowers on the chest
of drawers in front of the mirror. From
the other side, you're looking at me. I'm
looking at you. We smile at each other. I
walk towards the bed to give Isabelle the
reply Céline wrote her. Isabelle's staring
at the ceiling with her mouth open. I put
the letter in Isabelle's limp hand. You go
up on the stage and walk towards Céline
to give her Isabelle's last letter.

MANAGER, COSMETICS
SALESPERSON *and* DISPLAY
ASSISTANT *stop smiling.*

Céline opens the letter and reads it.
Céline's crying. She looks at you and
says: 'Thank you,' but without saying
thank you, just mouthing the words
'Thank you.' She takes your hand and
turns back to the audience. And there
you are, really alone – with Céline. And
you feel really good.

MANAGER, COSMETICS
SALESPERSON *and* DISPLAY
ASSISTANT *scrunch their eyes shut.*
ORACLE *smiles.*

Always do.

Long pause. Blackout.

CARYL CHURCHILL

Caryl Churchill has written for the stage, television and radio. Her stage plays include *Owners* (Royal Court Theatre Upstairs, 1972); *Objections to Sex and Violence* (Royal Court, 1975), *Light Shining in Buckinghamshire* (Joint Stock on tour incl. Theatre Upstairs, 1976); *Vinegar Tom* (Monstrous Regiment on tour, incl. Half Moon and ICA, 1976); *Traps* (Theatre Upstairs, 1977); *Cloud Nine* (Joint Stock on tour incl. Royal Court, London, 1979, then Theatre de Lys, New York, 1981); *Three More Sleepless Nights* (Soho Poly and Theatre Upstairs, 1980); *Top Girls* (Royal Court London, then Public Theater, New York, 1982); *Fen* (Joint Stock on tour, incl. Almeida and Royal Court, London, then Public Theatre, New York, 1983); *Softcops* (RSC at the Pit, 1984); *A Mouthful of Birds* with David Lan (Joint Stock on tour, incl. Royal Court, 1986); *Serious Money* (Royal Court and Wyndham's, London, then Public Theater, New York, 1987); *Icecream* (Royal Court, 1989); *Mad Forest* (Central School of Speech and Drama, then Royal Court, 1990); *Lives of the Great Poisoners* with Orlando Gough and Ian Spink (Second Stride on tour, incl. Riverside Studios, London, 1991); *The Skriker* (Royal National Theatre, 1994); *Thyestes* translated from Seneca (Royal Court Theatre Upstairs, 1994); *Hotel* with Orlando Gough and Ian Spink (Second Stride on tour, incl. The Place, London, 1997); *This is a Chair* (London International Festival of Theatre at the Royal Court, 1997); *Blue Heart* (Joint Stock on tour, incl. Royal Court Theatre, 1997); *Far Away* (Royal Court Theatre Upstairs, 2000, and Albery, London, 2001, then New York Theatre Workshop, 2002); *A Number* (Royal Court Theatre Downstairs, 2002, then New York Theatre Workshop, 2004); *A Dream Play* after Strindberg (Royal National Theatre, 2005); *Drunk Enough to Say I Love You?* (Royal Court Theatre Upstairs, 2006, then Public Theater, New York, 2008); *Bliss*, translated from Olivier Choinière (Royal Court Theatre, 2008).

OLIVIER CHOINIÈRE

Olivier founded the L'ACTIVITÉ Theatre Company in 2000 for which he has written and directed extensively. His theatre work includes *Félicité* (Théâtre La Licorne, 2007); *Bienvenue (À une Ville dont Vous Êtes le Touriste)* (Théâtre La Licorne, 2005); *Venise-en-Québec* (Théâtre d'Aujourd'hui, 2005); *Jocelyne est en Depression* (Théâtre d'Aujourd'hui, 2002); *Autodafé, Bûcher Historique en Cinq Actes* (Théâtre La Chapelle, 1999); *Le Bain des Raines* (Bain St Michel, 1999). His French-language translations of English plays include *Les Points Tournants (Passing Places)* by Stephen Greenhorn; *Howie le Rookie (Howie the Rookie)* by Mark O'Rowe; and *Road* by Jim Cartwright. *Félicité* was first written during the CEAD and Théâtre La Licorne Residencies, which Olivier took part in during 2004. He subsequently took part in the Royal Court's International Residency for Emerging Writers in London in 2007.